Life
in the
Middle

Finding God's Purpose in
the Midst of Uncontrollable Events

Tammy Harper

urbanpress

Life in the Middle: Finding God's Purpose
in the Midst of Uncontrollable Events
Copyright © 2017 Tammy Harper

ISBN 978-1-63360-061-4
For Worldwide Distribution
Printed in the U.S.A.

Urban Press
P.O. Box 8881
Pittsburgh, PA 15221-0881
412.646.2780
www.urbanpress.us

To all the mothers who have given birth or will give birth to a special needs child or children. May God grant you the strength and grace to raise your child with dignity and compassion.

Foreword

Tammy Harper was one of the first people I met when I came to Allegheny Center Alliance Church (ACAC) in 2000. Her daughter, Lydia, and many other children with special needs were in my class when I served as a lead teacher in the ACAC Children's Ministry for children three and four years old. I didn't have much contact with Tammy other than the brief time we would chat when she dropped off Lydia. Even in our brief encounters, however, I sensed she was a woman of strength and courage.

Lydia was a quiet and polite child, and always happy to come to class. When I shared that with Tammy, she seemed surprised and smiled, sometimes looking like she would cry. From then on, I always felt the need to share that with Tammy to encourage her, but little did I know until I read this book all the trauma and heartache she was experiencing in her own life.

God was preparing Tammy back then to use her today as a beacon of light to her children, her family, and many others who will read this wonderful and inspiring book. Only God knew when I first met Tammy what He was preparing her to do and be, and her story is destined to help many others who are in the middle of their own darkness, suffering, and pain.

Tammy has weathered the storms and proven herself to be a true woman of God. I'm inspired and encouraged by her story and was moved to tears as I read, discovering many things I did not previously know. She is a woman of faith in our Lord and Savior, Jesus Christ, and you will be challenged to raise your own faith level as you read about Tammy's. I know I was.

Tammy, you don't ever need to move away from the "middle." You have remained faithful and true in the place where our Lord has placed you – "in the middle" to be a bridge for those who need to access your faith and wisdom.

Be blessed, my dear sister, and know that you have been, and will continue to be, a blessing to many.

Sheran Zellous White
Founder & Executive Director
Five James Foundation

Introduction

I work in a field that requires a significant amount of compassion, patience, and a non-judgmental attitude toward those with whom we work. I need to have what we call in the industry "soul skills," which are to be silent, observe, understand, and listen. I just turned 50 years of age and if you were a part of my life years ago as a friend or family member, you would definitely say I did not possess those attributes.

I don't have a college degree. Instead, I learned what I know the hard way, through my own personal experience. You see, I have two children with multiple and complicated special needs. When I go into a home for work, I can sense what the families are going through, because I have gone through something similar myself. I work with colleagues who have college degrees, and I respect them so much. They are wonderful, dedicated professionals. My education, however, came through being "home schooled."

I have spoken on several occasions at my church to our ladies' group about my story and what I have been through. It was actually through my church that I found my job, for at church I came upon a brochure about the organization where I work. After I worked there a while, I was asked to tell my story at an event my agency holds annually. All the staff and leadership were there, and anyone in the mental health community along with the families served were also invited to attend.

I felt honored, first of all, that they would ask me to do that, but it really didn't surprise me that they asked me to do so. Years ago when my sister was killed, I spoke to my pastor after she had passed away and told him about a vision I had that God was going to use her situation to help other people. He was going to use who I had been and what I had been through to speak to those people. At that time, I could not even think about speaking to any group where I would eventually work, but I believed the Lord would prepare me, and He did. When I did address my colleagues at work, I didn't have a lot of fear, just a little bit of nerves. He prepared me and gave me the words, so it was not a problem.

My CEO and all of the people who supported me most and with whom I work side-by-side were all sitting there and crying. My supervisor said how proud she was of me and that she couldn't believe how much I had grown since I started working there.

That got me thinking that if my speaking could reach people with my story, then a book could do so as well. The Lord has put things in my heart to share for quite some time, things to help other families get through whatever they are encountering. I tell people that I have a Romans 8:28 job and life and Romans

8:28 says, "And we know that in all things God works for the good of those who love him, who have been called according to his purpose." What I have gone through will be used to help others, and it is my purpose in life to stand with them.

In this book, I am going to tell you about my life prior to my children, before I got my job, and before my first marriage. Yes, I have been married more than once. I have made many mistakes in my life, and I am going to share some of them with you. There is obviously some risk when I do this. After you are finished reading, you may think I am in no position to help anyone. You may consider my faith to be faulty or flawed. If you know me, you may look at me differently after you read this book.

That is the risk I am willing to take, however, because I don't believe I am the only one out there who has some problems, some of my own making and others that occurred because life just happened. At this point, I am not that concerned about what you think. I am simply looking for that drowning man or women to whom I can throw a life preserver and say, "It's alright. I understand; but better than that, God understands and He is with you. He wants to help you."

Through all my trials and tribulations, God has been with me. He has comforted me and given me hope and consolation. He has given my life purpose and has poured out His grace on me and my family. My church has stood with me, as have so many of my church and family members. I have much to be thankful for. I settled a long time ago that I am not worthy of God's love, yet He loves me anyway.

I have titled my book *Life in the Middle*, because it seems that I have been living in the middle of something my entire life—the middle of confusion, family fights, sick and distressed children, financial turmoil, and personal loss and setbacks. I wish I could say I am not in the middle of anything as I write, but I am. I am in the midst of a marriage conflict. I have asked the Lord, "What did I do wrong? Why this again?" and I am in counseling. You'll hear more about that later, but I wanted you to understand the rationale for the title. I think it is an accurate banner that should hang over the story of my life.

I invite you to come with me on a journey that will allow me to share with you how life's circumstances and uncontrollable events have taught me to glorify God and fulfill my purpose. As I was editing this introduction, I remembered a quote from Pastor Ed Glover when he said, "God's life for us is not for success but for significance." I do not consider my life a success by any stretch of the imagination, but I hope God will use my story in a significant way to help you as you read.

The book is called *Life in the Middle*, but we will start at the beginning. I will do my best to bring you up to the present as quickly as possible. Along the way, we will take a look at what God has taught me and is teaching me in the hopes that it will help you. If nothing else, you will know how to pray for me if God brings me to mind. Having said all that, let's get started.

Tammy Harper
Pittsburgh, PA
April 2017

Chapter 1
A Quick Overview

I am a Pittsburgher. We lived in the West End of the city in an area called Sheraden where my father had a business. When our first house we lived in caught fire, my father bought a farm in Washington County since he was a farm boy from Linesville, PA. We moved to that farm and I lived there until I was five years old. My mother was not too happy there since it required a lot of work on her part. Just to get water for all of us, she had to walk a distance to the spring house. Therefore, we kept that Washington County property and moved back into the city where we lived until I was in seventh or eighth grade. We ended up moving back out to the farm after my parents had a house built on the property, one that was more conducive to family living.

My twin brother and I helped my dad build that house in Washington County. By that time, there were four children at home with me and seven children altogether. You see, I was part of a blended family. My dad was married before and had one child. My mother was married before and had two. After my parents got married to each other, they had four kids, and I and my twin brother made up half of those four. Dad said whoever wanted a bedroom in that country house had better help him build it.

I made sure I was there because I couldn't stand having to share my bedroom. You might say I was a picky, neat-freak OCD little girl. My older sister was just the opposite and since she would have been my roommate, I made sure I was on the job at the building site. It was actually fun, as Dad showed me how to put tile and flooring in. I did all that and I worked the farm, which wasn't really a working farm, because Dad had a business in town. We did have cows and some crops my mother used for cooking. I stayed at that house and graduated from a school out by the farm.

My father died when I was 16, and my mother was a stay-at-home mom and didn't even drive. We drove her everywhere she went. She stayed in the city of Pittsburgh a lot with her parents to finalize all kinds of affairs after Dad died. My twin and I lived on the farm by ourselves for a year and a half so we could graduate while Mom bought and lived in a townhouse in the city of Pittsburgh. Mom took my younger sister with her so she could finish up in the City schools.

My brother and I were the only ones to graduate high school of all his kids. During the last few months of our senior year, my brother had to finish school in the city. Therefore, I was the only one who graduated high school and walked in a commencement ceremony. Knowing what I know now, I look back and see that we were all going through a lot after my dad's death. My brother was the only boy. Dad told my brother that he would have all that farmland when Dad died, but my mother sold it before that happened. Mom did the best she knew to do, but it was hard, and I think all of us look back and wish some decisions would have been made differently.

While in high school, I went to a vocational-technology school for cosmetology to get my license to do hair. I had my permit to do hair before I got my high school diploma, because I never missed school. I went on to make my living doing hair until my oldest child was six or seven years old. I had a large clientele from the community in which I grew up, which was the West End/Sheraden area. When I was 19 or 20, I left that area because I felt my business would never grow there. I thought I should go to a neighborhood where the per capita income was a bit higher. So I left a good following, taking a few clients with me, and went with a company where I assisted the established hairdressers while they gave me a chance to build my clientele. Within eight months of being in the South Hills, I had a full booking and stayed there for years.

After that, a few of us from that salon went somewhere else and I learned a lot about barbering, and that enabled me to share what I learned with others, which made me valuable to have around. Eventually, I had more men clients than women, and had a healthy following, but eventually left it because I felt the Lord called me to do so. I had surrendered my life to the Lord while working there and going through my first divorce. Samantha, my oldest daughter, was having all kinds of health issues, which I will explain later. I thought it was because I had to spend more time being a mom to care for her. Now I realize it was God teaching me. I was so new in the Lord and had a lot to learn.

I wasn't raised in a Christian home, but I know God had His hand on me. As I look back now, I see there were different things that happened and people who came into my life who could only have been from the Lord. For instance, there was one time my younger sister had a girlfriend over, and her mother came to pick her up. This woman started spewing all kinds of strange things, like the world was coming to an end and Jesus was coming back soon. I had never heard anything like that, and was totally intrigued. She was kind of crazy, but there was something compelling about what she was saying. I also remember my sister, who is two years older than I, being horrible to me, so bad that I would go into my closet in my bedroom and pray.

Then one day my mother said, "Tammy, I know a lady who goes to church, and I think you would like going with her. Why don't you go?" I went to this Baptist church in Crafton where they had a midweek program called Joy Club. Every Sunday from then on, this family took me to church and brought me home. I got my younger sister to go with me on Tuesdays to Joy Club and some Sundays to church.

People in the neighborhood would come around and invite us to church. I remember church puppet plays in the neighborhood outside my home. Then at times, a school bus came to pick all the kids up to take us to church. There was a young couple in the neighborhood who invited us into their home for singing and worship.

When I lived in Avella where I went to high school, my girlfriend who lived down the road invited me to come and attend Sunday School with her and her family. Now I understand the truth behind the verse in 1 John 4:19, "We love because he first loved us." God was reaching out to me for almost my entire young life!

That's a quick summary of what I remember from those earliest years. Since I turned 50 as I write, and since this first chapter summarizes my earliest years of life, I will break down the rest of my life in ten-year chunks, and with that, let's move on to finish up the look into my first ten years of life.

Chapter 2
More About My Family

It's a challenge to reconstruct the early years of one's life. The memories start to blur and blend together, so that what I remember may not be how another family member recalls the same period or circumstances. I know some family members may read this and remember things differently. I can only share what I remember, but I fully acknowledge that my memory may be a bit faulty or my perspective limited—or just different.

Before Mom married my dad, she gave birth to two girls: Juanita and Margaret. We called Juanita "Wandy" and we called Margaret Peggy. My dad, from a previous marriage, had a daughter Kathleen, who later in life changed her name to Renee. After my parents got married, they had four kids: Donna is my older natural sister two years older than I, my twin brother Thomas and me, and Priscilla, a younger sister by three years. Growing up, it was always my two older sisters and us four. We didn't see much of my sister Kathleen (Renee), but later as young adults we got to know each other better.

My dad was a go-getter, probably what we would today call a workaholic. Dad grew up on a farm in Linesville, PA. I believe it was his father or grandfather who started the Yellow Cab union here in Pittsburgh. His dad's nickname was Happy, and he was a self-proclaimed doctor. I guess he prescribed various wellness treatments and natural types of prescriptions, and was a jack-of-all-trades.

Dad was not at home a lot, and my mother was a full-time housewife. She didn't have a formal education, but she raised us and worked very hard in her own right. I mentioned in the last chapter that Dad bought a farm and Mom felt stranded when we lived there. She didn't drive, and on the farm we lived down in the valley where Mom didn't see anyone but her kids. Dad worked out of town a lot as a truck and cab driver.

Dad would befriend men who worked with him and bring them home to stay with us. Eventually, they would leave and go back to work. Sometimes they would bring home kids who were related to them and Mom became the caregiver for them all. My father slowly built up his trucking business, even when we moved back to Pittsburgh after Mom got fed up with life on the farm. Eventually he bought property in the West End for his company, Parkway Trucking, because our neighbors didn't like all the noise of the trucks at our house. Dad called me his little girl and Miss America. Mom knew he favored me for whatever reason, and Mom favored Thom, her only son.

Even though we weren't brought up in a home of faith, Mom told me that we were baptized as infants. My dad's mom, who I don't remember, belonged to an Episcopalian church in the West End and that's where we were baptized. Wandy, my older sister who was like my second mother, supposedly taught the kids Sunday School and I was always on her hip. My mother said I was always with Wandy, and I called her Nonny. My mother didn't know she was having twins until she was seven months pregnant. Up to that point, she had all girls, and everyone wanted a boy.

My mom told some nuns at the hospital that she wanted a boy and that she couldn't accept another girl. I was born first and she said if the next one was a girl, she didn't want it! The nuns said they would pray, but it was already decided, and thankfully, it was a boy. When I was younger, it bothered me that she didn't want me! Sometimes parents don't know how painful things like that can be for their children. In part, that's why I was so close with my older sister, who was 12 years older than I.

My mother says that I was Wandy's baby doll, so she took care of me and we were really close. My brother was definitely the star of the family being the only boy. As I matured, my mother noticed something in me and always told me that I liked all that "church stuff." Mom started bowling with a lady down the street who was always talking about Jesus. Mom sent me to church with this woman, and for many years I went to a Baptist church with that woman and her family.

I was the only one in the family who went, although I had my younger sister go with me from time to time. I got up by myself early Sunday morning, made breakfast, watched cartoons, and got ready to go to church, wearing the same dress most Sundays. I was embarrassed that it was the same dress, but I didn't care that much because I wanted to go to church. I don't know why I stopped going, but I think it was my interest in boys that began to occupy my time.

Looking back, I wish I had more family support in my

church interest, but I didn't. Perhaps it would have kept me from making some of the poor decisions I went on to make. As I lived and grew up in Sheraden, it was a predominately white community, but over the hill from where I lived there was a black community. That didn't bother me, but my family seemed to have a problem with it. I heard things from them about black people that hurt my heart.

I remember watching things like the mini-series *Roots*, which gave a picture of slavery in America. I would sit real close to the television when I watched TV because my eyesight was poor, and my mother would make fun of me for it. That series was very meaningful for me. Let me say as an aside that I attend a church today that has a healthy percentage of black worshippers and I feel right at home. Also, I work with quite a diverse group of families on my job. God was preparing my heart even as a child to be open to all people, and that has certainly enriched my life and helped me in my work and ministry.

I liked school, but I had bad grades in first grade and think I failed. They held my brother back and because we were twins, they held me back, too. I was upset the next year at having to repeat, but from then on, I was on the honor roll all the way through school. Having to repeat that year was actually to my benefit.

When I got a little older and more in tune with my environment, I fought a lot with my parents, especially my mom because she was the one who was around. My dad wasn't a drinking man because his dad had been an alcoholic. My grandfather died when he got drunk, fell, and hit his head on a curb. Later in life, I surmised that Dad had an eye for women and was a workaholic instead of an alcoholic. My mom would be sick but he would not stay home. Instead, he would have a babysitter come over so he could go out. I know that was a heartache for my mother.

When we owned the farm, there were times we had renters and there were times we didn't. My dad would go out to the farm on weekends and take us with him to work on it. In the summers, we would have our vacations there while he worked on the farm, and I loved it. It was a big farm with a pond, a chicken coop, spring house (for water), and a pigpen. When we were only visiting and not living there, we didn't have the animals. There was a barn and a silo, and I thought it was beautiful.

I continued to be close with Wandy, but then one day when she was about 19, she wasn't around any longer. I was only seven, and I didn't understand what had happened. The same thing happened with Peggy. There were arguments in our living room with all kinds of yelling and screaming between my sisters and parents.

My parents were saying something about going up to the front street and hanging out and they were not to go up there. They would call my sisters bad-girl names, accusing them of doing this and that, and carrying on with the boys. Wandy did end up getting pregnant at a young age. She was 19 when she had her first child and my aunt helped her make it on her own. My other sister ran off with her boyfriend to get married.

So Wandy was gone and we kept going to school, and then one day she appeared with a toddler. I had never seen a baby or toddler, except my younger sister. My mother informed me that the baby was my niece. That was hard for me to understand, for Wandy had disappeared and then came back with a baby that was only eight years younger than I. Wandy and Peggy got older and of course so did I, but I missed Wandy and in some ways never replaced her in my life. That brings me up to my teen years, so let's move on to the next ten-year segment of my life that would take me through being a teenager into young adulthood.

Chapter 3
The Teen Years: Growing Up Too Fast

I am naturally blond, but I help it along now, for you know how things change as we get older! My twin brother, however, has brown hair and brown eyes. My mom and dad called me the blond-headed witch just to tease me. Then my dad would say I would be Miss America one day. You can say I was getting mixed signals that produced a conflicted self-image.

I was always scared in Greenway Middle School because the kids were so mean and rotten. I learned things there I didn't need to learn, like how to fight. I had to learn how to be mean and nasty and pretend like I was the bad city girl, which was really a façade. I knew if I looked frightened, they would keep after me, and my strategy worked.

Knowing what got my older sisters into trouble, my parents decided to move back to Washington County and build a new house on the farm property to try and keep me and my younger siblings out of the same trouble. A new house was the only way Mom was going to move back there. I tell dads who have a daughter to pay attention to her as she gets older. Sometimes when dads see their young teen girls maturing, they tend to back away, because they don't know what to do with them and they figure that girls are mom's area of expertise. Those teen years are the most vulnerable age for a girl, and she often wants a father to come into her life and love on her. If that doesn't occur, they can go out and look for their love and affirmation from someone else.

As I mentioned, we had tenants who lived right on top of the lane near the farm for many years, and they were really good friends with my dad. They would keep my dad informed of what was going on there, and they turned our property into a beautiful, working farm. I already reported that when my dad started building, he said that if the kids wanted their own bedroom, they'd have to come help build it. I was at the point in our old city house that I would live in the attic because I hated sharing my room with sisters. It was hot in the summer and cold in the winter in the attic, and it was generally creepy, but I didn't care.

I cleaned that attic, had a radio and a lamp, and I was good to go. I froze, but I didn't care because it was my own room and my own space. The incentive to go help and build my own room was strong when Dad made the offer. By then I had a boyfriend, so he told me to bring him along so Dad could get to know him. My brother also went down to the farm a lot. One weekend Dad showed me how to tile a bathroom, but most of the time, I was his gopher. My older sister, Donna, didn't come, so she had to share a room with our younger sister Priscilla, and she hated it. She didn't want to move down from Pittsburgh, however, which is why she didn't want to help. She was 16 and more established in her friendships, so it was more difficult for her to move.

Before we moved out to the country and before I was interested in boys at the age of 12 or 13, I loved to roller skate. I had no way of getting to the rink, however, because my dad wasn't around and my mother didn't drive. So my brother-in-law agreed to take me and bring me back home in return for babysitting my sister's children. To my horror, my brother-in-law made a pass at me one day as we were driving home. He pulled into an alley and tried to take advantage of me. Thank God I wasn't too far from home because I opened the door and ran.

I brooded all night and finally talked to my mother about it. My mother called my sister Wandy and made me get on the phone to report what happened to her. I felt like I was destroying someone's life. Later that day, I found out from Donna that he tried the same thing with her. Years later, Wandy was still with him and he tried the same things with my younger sister. All that somehow got swept under the carpet, and I moved out into the country where I didn't have to see them all very often. My mother told me not to tell my father because he would kill my sister's husband. I listened to my mother, because I didn't want anyone to get hurt. I carried that incident in my mind for years, feeling guilty for what had happened and for having to tell my sister. I was too young to know how they lived with or resolved that issue.

After a few years, I would stay with my sister on weekends, thinking my brother-in-law would behave. Once they went to a wedding while I watched the kids, staying over after they got home. I was 15 or 16 years old, and was sleeping on the couch when he made the same advances in the middle of the night. I started screaming, and left their home right then and there. He chased me down the street, asking me not to tell my sister because she would take his daughter away from him. I am now trained to understand the trauma that such incidents cause, but I had no such information back then, and I carried that guilt and confusion for many years.

I attended Avella High School when we lived on the farm, and I had a good experience there. I liked it in the country, but I hated that my boyfriend lived in the city. We dated on the weekends and any other time we could. Being apart from each other produced an unhealthy, dysfunctional relationship, and it was not God-honoring in any way.

My high school was small and I graduated with 63 seniors. I liked it because I didn't have to watch to see if someone was going to throw something at me, or if I was going to be attacked at lunch or grabbed in the hallway like was happening in the city school (that had happened to me when I was in the seventh grade before we moved).

My main problem at that point in life was the little faith and knowledge of God I had both disappeared. The only little glimpse of faith going on in my world was when I moved to Washington and made friends with a girl down the road. Her mom and dad went to a small Christian church deep in the woods, and I would always ask if they were going to church. I would get in the truck with her and her dad, which had the gear shift on the steering wheel, which seemed so strange to me. The pastor would preach and we would go to Sunday School in a one-room church.

Mom was happier the second time around on the farm because our home was a lot bigger. She was a wonderful mother, keeping up with the kids, and an excellent homemaker. Unfortunately, there wasn't much of a relationship between Dad and her. Dad would travel into the city every other day and stay with my godparents; my godfather was working for Dad. Dad would come on weekends and jump right onto his tractor.

We had some good times as a family on the weekends. One funny story I remember is when Dad had me clean out the silo, and there was years and years of fermented corn piled high in the silo. My cousin Kim and I were able to climb on top of the corn pile, where we took pitchforks, opened the big back door, and starting pitching out the corn. We ended up lying flat on our backs, laughing hysterically by the time Dad came in and found us. We were high because of the fumes from the corn that had fermented and became like moonshine. We didn't know what was happening to us, but Dad was yelling for us to get out. We were stoned, but Dad sent us to shovel the crap out of the barn, and that seemed to sober us up.

I studied to become a cosmetologist through a vocational-tech program in high school. The teacher had two openings in the program the year I was eligible. It seemed like half the class of girls were interested in doing hair. I never thought about college, only hair. The teacher asked me if I wanted to do it, so I said, "Sure, why not?" I went to cosmetology classes in the morning and school in the afternoon. I did that for a few years and then went on to earn my cosmetology manager's license. From there, I went to work at a salon.

Actually I worked in the summer, since Dad had property in the city. My boyfriend was there and my older sisters lived in Pittsburgh as well and had their own lives. My one sister was married and had another little girl. I would come in on weekends and holidays and had a job assisting in a salon when I was only 16. I started working for money at 12 as a babysitter and at 13 at my dad's garage in the summer, sweeping all of the stuff off the floor. I liked to make money and to be able to spend it.

When I was 14, I remember Dad got me a job in Sheraden at a delicatessen called The Little Store.

Then the unexpected happened. My father died when I was 16 and in tenth grade, and that was a traumatic event. My sister Donna, who married at age 17, had left her husband and moved back to the farm while they tried to work things out to get back together again. One night on Valentine's Day, we were at the house on the farm, and I went to bed. My mother woke me up, saying that something had happened to my father and someone was coming to pick me up to take me to the hospital. Later that night, Donna came in and told me to get some things together because we were going to spend some time in the city to be near Dad and with Mom. She drove us to my godparents' home in the West End, and that's when we found out something was wrong.

It was 4 AM and everyone was awake, sitting around the table having coffee with a somber and distressed look because they knew they had to tell us. My mother finally shared that my dad died of a heart attack. I remember falling back into a chair. My brother actually ran outside and down the street, and my uncle had to go chase him down. To Thom, Dad was his world. My dad was 50 when this happened. Of course, the next few days were traumatic for my mother, and for all of us, for that matter. We had to go to my grandparents, and the only way to get there was to drive past my dad's business in the West End.

I knew that death was a part of life, but it was a tough few years. Mom didn't work, and she didn't know about business and finances. Her world was turned upside down. She eventually dealt with it all over the next year, and ended up moving back to the city where she bought a townhouse in Sheraden. Thom and I lived on the farm to finish our senior year at Avella. I went to school and did my thing, but my brother ended up back in Pittsburgh.

After Dad died, I had to take my mother shopping because she didn't drive. On the trip when we were shopping for her funeral dress, Mom said for the first time I could recall that she loved me. It was in the Kaufmann's Department Store changing room. It was awkward and uncomfortable, but she was grateful for me being there. Ever since then, Mom's always called me to do this and that. I'm not complaining but it made me feel so responsible for her after Dad died. I felt that made me grow up too fast. My siblings helped a lot, but it felt like I was the one she went to when she needed something.

In my junior year and the year after Dad died, I found out I was pregnant, and I was scared to death to tell my mother. I started having problems and was bleeding. My mother was in the city dealing with my dad's estate. My girlfriend was with me and my boyfriend took the two of us to the hospital. They told me that I was so many weeks along. Then I had no choice but to tell Mom and she flipped out. I was distraught over how she reacted and how she treated me. She actually had my older sister try to talk me into having an abortion. I just didn't want to do that but didn't know what else to do. I was confused, but God was merciful. Prior to that happening, I miscarried and found that I had been carrying twins.

I felt like I betrayed God and that He was going to kill me. Looking back, God knew what He had planned for me in the future. He knew I couldn't handle those two children, and do what He wanted me to do later in life. After I lost the children, I had to forgive my mother and forgive myself. I had to forgive myself for allowing her to push me to the point where I considered an abortion. It was a long time before I could truly forgive her, because I didn't understand how she could act like it was nothing. It's something I still need to talk about with her, because I just want and need her to know.

At the same time, I look back now and realize how rebellious and self-willed I was. As I reflect today, Psalm 25 takes on new and special meaning for me. The psalm reads: "Remember, Lord, your great mercy and love, for they are from of old. Do not remember the sins of my youth and my rebellious ways; according to your love, remember me, for you, Lord, are good" (Psalm 25:6-7).

That completes the story of my teen years, which ushered into my next ten years as a young adult. It was then that I made many poor choices, and some life things happened that were difficult to process. Let's look at those years now, for they all contribute to my story of God's faithfulness as I lived the middle of life's pain.

Chapter 4
My First Marriage

After graduation, I worked in a salon for a few years after serving as a salon assistant in the West End. When I first moved back to the city, I found out my longtime boyfriend was addicted to drugs. I knew he had some issues, but I didn't realize how deep they were, so we broke up. Unfortunately, because of the girl I was then, I went with another boyfriend right away and he had his own set of problems. My old boyfriend didn't just go away, however, for he had been part of the family for many years. He looked up to my father because his father wasn't involved in his life.

I came home late one night and as a friend dropped me off, my old boyfriend was lurking nearby. He suddenly appeared and dragged me into a car. First, he beat me and then raped me. We had driven over an hour north into the country and he just left me there in the middle of the night. Eventually he came back and drove me home. Who could I tell? Who would listen because we had been together for so long? Of course, that event was also traumatic. I remember being heartbroken and getting into my car to go to my dad's grave site to talk to him. "Dad, what do I do?" I didn't really know the Lord at the time, but I felt the Lord's presence during everything I went through.

I often think about God's mercy toward me in my early years. I had so much pain and did not know how to reach out and get help before I went in the wrong direction. I was trying to be the good girl because of something in me, while living in denial of my sin. That is how I ushered in the life decade of my twenties.

I met another boyfriend when he was dating my friend. We were all out one night and my friend drank a bit too much, so we took her home, and then he and I spent some time talking. He seemed like a good guy with a good heart and we got married eventually. I met him when I was 19. He was a bit older and was divorced before we met. We got married when I was 24 and at 27 I gave birth to my daughter Samantha.

We struggled for a bit when we first got married, and we were living in an apartment. I got a job outside of the Pittsburgh area in the South Hills, but in doing that, I had to start all over to obtain a new clientele. My oldest sister, Wandy, and her two daughters lived in Bridgeville at the time, though she and her husband were separated. Since Wandy worked nights and Bridgeville was closer to where my job was, we went to live with her. The deal was my husband would fix up the basement as a bedroom for my older niece (so we could use her room) and we would help Wandy care for the girls while she worked at night. Eventually we were able to save up enough money to rent an apartment of our own in that area.

We continued to save and soon we were able to purchase a townhouse back in the city, right across from my mother. My husband was a carpenter and remodeled our home. He was often injured during our marriage and was in a lot of accidents. It seemed like he was constantly in and out of surgery.

After I had Samantha and was going through all of the struggles with her (more on that in the next chapter), he hurt his knee and after many months, he went back to work. A month or two later, he was hurt in a bad accident in his new vehicle when a big delivery truck hit him while he was stopped at a light. His head went forward and then back and he smashed the back window of his truck. There were no cuts, however, and he walked away from the accident. I wondered why they didn't keep him in the hospital for observation. It turned out he reinjured his knee and had to have surgery on it again. For more than a year, he couldn't go back to work because of the pain in his back. The doctors reported that there was nothing wrong with him and thought he was faking an injury.

Finally, he went to a different specialist who found a hairline fracture in his back. When they realized he wasn't faking and required surgery, they fused his back with screws. That was significant because then we went through a lawsuit to be eligible for worker's compensation, since he was out of work and was wearing a harness on his back. There I was, taking Samantha to tend to all of her needs, taking care of him, and at the same time working in the salon. Thank God for my mother, because she would come and help out.

My husband and I went through a rough time and fought a lot after that. What he was saying often didn't make any sense. Basically, he wasn't the same man I had married. With the latest information about concussions, I now know that he had a severe and traumatic brain injury that changed the way he thought and how he behaved. At the time, we didn't know that.

My husband bought me a beautiful dining room set, and then he packed up and left us. I remember Samantha at three years old watching her father and his friend move all his stuff. That was a tough time. Then I got caught up in a different relationship and things got worse. Finally, I got to the point where I could not deal with the pressures of life and a special-needs child. Eventually, I started going to my girlfriend's church in the South Hills at the invitation of the man I was dating. When I started listening to the sermons, I realized my relationship with that man was ungodly, and I had to leave the church after we broke up.

After I left, my other girlfriends kept telling me about a church on the North Side of Pittsburgh. Finally, I was feeling so empty and alone that I just picked up the phone, dialed information, and told the operator that I was looking for a church on the North Side. Since Allegheny Center Alliance Church (ACAC) is one of the first churches listed alphabetically, that is the number the operator gave me—the number for ACAC. I doubt if she knew it was on the North Side. I called the church for directions and came to my first service.

I was a little overwhelmed, and just sat in a pew while Pastor Bruce Jackson was preaching. Some young ladies were watching me, and came up to me right after the service when I told them my story. One of those ladies took me around, showed me the children's ministry, and stopped in the hall where she started praying for me. I have been at that church ever since, and it has stood by me through all my trials since 1998.

A significant event of my first marriage was the birth of my firstborn daughter, Samantha, and it is important that I tell you about her at this point in this book's journey, so let's go there now.

Chapter 5
Samantha's Story

Much of my story of living in the middle is wrapped around my children and their needs. I will go into more detail later, but let me tell you now about Samantha, my oldest. Her dad and I were married about four years when we first started trying to get pregnant. When she was born, the hospital officials took her right away from me and felt something wasn't right. It took some time before a pediatrician came to tell me there was something wrong with my baby, but they weren't quite sure what it was. All they could see was that she had some skin problems. They eventually brought her to me, but said they were contacting Children's Hospital.

I freaked out because all I could hear was that something was wrong with my baby. My family was quite supportive, especially my older sister who was a nurse. When we brought Samantha home, she did okay for a while. We thought it was just a skin issue and that she was getting progressively better. Then she wasn't walking at 12 months, or 15 months, or 18, and then I was the one who kept telling the doctor something wasn't right. They finally sent us to Children's Hospital and the doctor reported that Sam had flat feet and would be fine. That didn't sit well with me. Some family members told me to go to a different doctor they had used previously.

I knew there were some problems when they brought in another specialist and had Samantha walking around, or at least what little walking she was able to do. At first, the doctors felt she may have some spasticity and weren't sure how severe it was. Then we had her in a study and 15 dermatologists were studying her at the same time, because they didn't know what kind of skin condition she had and didn't know what we needed to do for her.

Then she was sent to a neurologist, who said she needed an MRI. From that, they discovered she had what is called white matter on her brain. That indicated Samantha had some form of cerebral palsy. They assigned her a diagnosis of something called Lameler Ichthyosis, but then they discounted that diagnosis. I may sound scattered as I describe this time, and that's exactly what I was! I could not get any rational, definitive answers about what was wrong with my Samantha. It was frustrating and excruciating, and is still difficult to piece together to this very day.

Then one day at work, I was talking to a pediatrician who was a resident at Children's Hospital and he knew what we were going through at the time. He related to me that there was a baby who had just been born who had a really severe skin disorder, and we talked about that baby every time he came in to the shop. They said she looked like a monster, but it was actually a form of the skin disease that Sam had. The baby had an extremely rare and severe type of Ichthyosis. Sam's type is extremely rare, too.

Ironically, my own physician called me to tell me about that same baby the resident had mentioned to me. When I told my doctor that I had already heard about that child, he asked if I would be willing to talk to the baby's mom so we could encourage one another. That mom's name is Patty and she became a good friend.

Patty recommended that we make a trip to the National Institute of Health in Maryland where that they could possibly let us know for sure what was afflicting Sam. We got our hopes up for a correct diagnosis, only to be disappointed again when they told us that they really weren't sure what type of Ichthyosis she had. The specialist there called us at one point to inform us that a genetic doctor had recently discovered a gene for this rare specific type of disease and felt Sam should get some more tests. By this time, she was almost three.

We went for the testing and they discovered that Sam had this recently-discovered gene that led to the true diagnosis of her condition as Icthyosis SJogren-Larsson Syndrome. The doctors didn't know much about it, and had no explanation for it. There were three major symptoms of this type of Ichthyosis: intellectual challenges, dry and thickening skin, and spasticity. At least we then knew what we were dealing with and could begin treatments. They injected botox into different parts of her legs to help her walk as best she could. She has to be checked every year for retinitis because she could go blind with this particular disease. Samantha was the third confirmed case of this Icthyosis in the country at that time.

Poor little Sam didn't know what was going on. She is quite shy to this day, and I attribute that in part to her being poked and prodded so much when she was a baby. There were all kinds of people around her causing her pain, and her response was typical. She is a lot more outgoing now. To this day, she has to be treated regularly. She has to have long baths and have lotions and creams mixed with acid put on her to scrape off the skin. She needs constant skin care, but it's not painful. It's just an annoying process for someone in her condition.

Sam trained me to be patient and I was going to need every bit of that patience for my second daughter Lydia, who has some mental health challenges. When I compare having to care for a child with intellectual and medical issues as opposed to one with mental health issues, the mental health is much more challenging.

There is no question that Sam's medical condition contributed to the failure of my first marriage. I am not blaming Sam, for I love her; she is the joy of my life. But a husband and wife have to have strong relationship to weather the disability or death of a child. Those problems will test the foundation of any marriage, and our foundation could not stand up under the strain of the constant doctor's visits, uncertainties of what a day would bring, and the special care that required all our attention—attention that should and could have been devoted to one another.

One day, while talking and arguing, I looked at my husband and it was like a totally different person had taken over who he was. I am glad to report that he is better now. But at that time, we were two sinful people in a bad marriage with a child who had multiple disabilities. I later saw a study that showed 50% of all marriages today end in divorce, but that increases to 75% for a couple raising a child with a disability, and more than 80% when a couple is raising a child with a mental health disability.

My husband was supportive of Samantha by being there for her, even if he could not take her to her appointments. He did what he could to take care of her. During that time, we had an attorney for his injury, and the attorney advised us to sue the hospital over Sam's birth and her cerebral palsy because he thought the hospital was negligent in how they first handled her condition. I kept telling the attorney that I was doing the research to find out what was going on with her and finding the right answers.

I eventually discovered that her disorder was not from being born a few weeks or months early. It's a genetic condition that results in spasticity residing in the white matter of the brain (this was also the source of the skin disorder). It was not the result of an accident or trauma. There was nothing that happened that constituted liability on anyone's part; it was purely a genetic issue. My husband and his parents never wanted to own up to that. There was pride involved in that they didn't want to believe it was something in their blood line that had caused Sam's condition. They just wanted to blame other people. Sam's condition was the result of a one-in-a-million likelihood that Sam's father and I would have the genes to produce Sam's situation.

It was heartbreaking to take her to have the procedures while she was screaming in pain. I saw my little baby being tortured and it was traumatic. During the years of my first marriage, we both acted horribly. He got hooked on strip clubs, and I ended up having an affair, and he did as well. We went down the wrong path, both of us. Eventually we separated. We got the settlement money from his injury, but we ended up fighting the attorney to be able to settle. No one had any idea what I went through taking care of a child with a disability and him at the same time, and no one believing me about Sam's condition. This was around 1997.

Sam's father was more involved when she was younger, but hasn't been for many years. He lives in Cleveland and sees her maybe twice a year since he runs the road as a truck driver. It would be nice if he could be more involved, but he has his own life and I think he's doing the best that he can.

I met my second husband Joe at church after my divorce. I was just new to my faith and trying to understand my faith, and he pursued me. I started going to the singles groups while raising Sam and he stepped in, helping us out in many ways. This was around 1998 and Sam was about five or six years old. She still calls him Uncle Joe to this day. Eventually we dated and got married in 2000. Then a year later, I had Lydia. Five months after I got pregnant with Lydia, our marriage ran into serious problems, the details of which I would rather not discuss in this forum. Joe's daughter and son both lived with us, and I love them dearly to this day, but it was really bad. Joe is good with Sam now that he's dealt with some of his life challenges. He is a very good dad and is there for his kids.

We will talk more about all of these episodes and situations later. I am simply trying to give you an overview of my qualifications for the job I mentioned earlier. I want you to have a sense of what I have gone through—I was always living life in the middle of some crisis, some sickness, some broken relationship—and how faithful God has been to me. I also want to glorify God, and I desire to tell you where I have come from to see the place that God has brought me to today.

This story would not be complete without me sharing the psalm that came to mean so much to me as we walked through Samantha's diagnosis. That psalm is Psalm 139:13-14, "For it was you who created my inward parts, you knit me together in my mother's womb. I will praise you because I have been remarkably and wonderfully made. Your works are wonderful and I know this full well."

In spite of Samantha's physical challenges, I saw God's hand in it all. I knew He loved her and me, and that in spite of it all, God did not make a mistake. I held on to that truth, even when the evidence seemed to say something to the contrary. I am not saying I saw all that in the early days, but as I look back, I see the truth in those verses more and more. My Samantha was and is wonderfully made, and I love her very much. Now let me tell you about my little Lydia, my second-born daughter.

Chapter 6
Loving Lydia

As I explained in the Introduction, I titled this book *Life in the Middle* because it seems that's where I have always been—in the middle of something. One of the things I learned as a Christian is that we are often in the middle of something called spiritual warfare. This warfare is with unseen forces that assail our lives and the lives of our loved ones to steal our joy and take away our life energy. I have come to rely on a passage in 2 Corinthians 10:3-5, which states,

> For though we walk in the flesh, we are not wag-
> ing war according to flesh. For the weapons of our
> warfare are not of the flesh, but have divine power
> to destroy strongholds. We destroy arguments and
> every lofty opinion against the knowledge of God,
> and take every thought captive to obey Christ.

At times I have felt like I was in the middle of a hurricane. Yet while in prayer, I felt like I was in the eye of the storm, looking through it at my storm all around me and having unexplainable peace. I have had to learn how to fight to maintain my peace, however, along with the welfare of my children, and for my ability to function on any given day—all while living in the middle of something, even in the middle of a hurricane.

When my second daughter Lydia was born, I had an easy and peaceful delivery. It was a beautiful experience. Months later, however, she started having problems. First, she began to get sick a lot as a toddler. She had viruses with temperatures of 105. She also started having a lot of behavioral issues. Then she started having other little problems, like an unusual movement of her mouth. She would talk and her whole jaw would go sideways. She couldn't figure out if she wanted something or not. I would give her a sippy cup that she wanted, and then she'd scream when she got it. She wouldn't sleep most of the night and it seemed like she was up for years. I kept telling anyone who would listen that something wasn't right.

I was nervous and concerned, and my family tried to comfort me, saying that I was worrying about her because of what I had been through with Sam. Her behaviors got progressively worse with constant tantrums and screaming—and that went on for hours. By this time, I was pregnant with my son Westin, who was born when Lydia was two years old.

Lydia didn't talk, so when someone told me about the Alliance for Infants and Toddlers, I had them come to my home and evaluate her. They said she definitely had speech delay, which I already knew, along with some occupational therapeutic problems. They attributed the fact that she had a hard time walking on her flat feet, so they tried to strengthen her legs with physical therapy. After a few months of coming and spending time with her, they recommended that a psychologist come in and have her evaluated.

Finally, she was diagnosed with autism spectrum disorder called PDD—Pervasive Developmental Disorder. That's a form of autism, but they stayed away from the autism label at the time because she was young and they wanted to address some of her other issues therapeutically. A speech pathologist felt she had apraxia, which affected how she talked. Then they determined she had dysarthria, which is what caused her jaw to go sideways. She received one diagnosis after another.

It got to the point where I had to take Lydia to Children's Hospital to have her evaluated. Then they found out she was having seizures. They gave her medication but it only made things worse, so I tried a diet change. Then they informed me that Lydia had several metabolic irregularities. I spent a lot of time on the phone with the specialists, taking her to get more therapy and trying to figure out what everything meant. It was difficult, especially when we were in public and people would look and stare like I was a bad parent. After all that, I decided to take her to a genetic doctor like I had done for Sam.

They sent all of the tests out to the Netherlands and said it would take nine months to figure out if she had what they thought she had. Thank God all that came back negative. They did report that she had Orotic Asiduria Syndrome, a metabolic disorder, for which there is no cure. She had some of the tendencies of that Syndrome but not all of them. I had many therapists and people coming in and out of the house. It felt like I wasn't running a home, I ran a facility. Lydia needed a lot of services, and I had to fight with the insurance companies to get the payments approved.

The doctors said it was a million to one odds that the genes between Sam's father and I would produce Sam's issues. With what Lydia has, the odds are a couple hundred thousand to one that her dad and I carried the genes to produce her condition.

When my third child was born, a boy we named Westin, he had years of mobile therapy that come in to work with all of us. Westin puts up with a lot. He knows the Lord, however, and he's an amazing young man. One day he is going to have a story to write as well.

I remember when Sam was a little one and I was still working as a stylist. I was going through a divorce and working as a single mom. I was depressed and knew I was falling into a pit. I knew I had to stay strong, so I decided to go volunteer at Children's Hospital to work with the babies. That may sound like unusual therapy, but it really helped me. I remember holding the babies and encountering a little girl who was eight or nine years old. She didn't have any arms or legs, and she had AIDS. I was pulling her around in a little wagon.

She was whining and crying, and the nurses were getting angry with her because her parents would just drop her off and then leave. God used that little girl to show me that I was going to be okay. That's what I needed to pull out of my funk. My friends thought I was nuts because of all I was going through at the time, the last thing I needed was to volunteer to be around children with problems.

About that time is when I found ACAC, my church. I was new in my faith and struggling. I had a few relationships during that time, and one was with a man who portrayed himself as godly, which he was not. When I saw who he really was, as I mentioned before, I knew I couldn't go back to the church he had taken me to in the South Hills.

This was when I called the operator and asked about the a church on the North Side and she gave me the information for ACAC. I went to the service that morning and have been there ever since. I told you that God has been faithful to me, leading me when I didn't even know He was around. In the next chapter, I want to talk more about that church, and the role it played in helping me survive living in the middle.

Chapter 7
Church Life

At that point in my life, I not only had my Lydia, but I also had my hands full with Sam. I had her in preschool at a young age, but had to make sure that where she was at was appropriate for her safety and learning. Sam had to have air conditioning due to her skin condition because she doesn't sweat properly, and consequently retains body heat. Thus, she can easily overheat and have a heatstroke. After her preschool, Sam enrolled in a public school.

Sam went through the Head Start and the Early Intervention Programs. They bussed her around and I would follow the bus to the schools to make sure everything was safe. I was constantly calling her school with concerns about her education to ensure that she was being cared for properly. The people at the special needs board knew me by my first name because I was contacting them so often.

Sam constantly had to have speech, occupational, and physical therapy. She spoke, but she was very shy. She could talk, but she was behind on her communication skills. If things were wrong, she really didn't say anything, so no one knew. As her mother, I knew her best and worked diligently to know what was going on, even when she could not communicate it for herself. As she got older, her speech improved greatly. A lot of her shyness stemmed from so many people hovering over her, trying to care for her, and she would become overwhelmed. As she got older, she also was able to walk a little bit with what we called her "magic shoes." They were like the leg braces that Forrest Gump wore in the movie by that name. She would also walk a little bit with her k-walker.

Later in life after my divorce, my brother came around one time and wanted us to go out. We went and I kept thinking, "What am I doing here?" I felt that I didn't need to be out where we were. I used to love the party and social scene, but for the first time, I knew I had to make some changes. Plus, as I attended church, I found myself craving knowledge and understanding of what God wanted from me and what the Bible said.

Sam loved the church. I started teaching two-year-olds on Wednesday nights, and she enjoyed the experience. I loved working with the little ones, and I learned a lot. I was at church all day long on Sunday, going from one class to another.

My family wasn't surprised that I was going to church, and some thought, "Oh, there goes Tammy. She always has God in her life." It didn't matter to me what they thought because I knew they saw positive changes in my life. Perhaps they looked at it like I was grasping at straws because of my life situation, and they would have been correct. They couldn't understand if I loved and served God so much, why didn't God do something about Sam's condition. I was reaching out for God like a drowning woman would a life preserver. I was a mess and needed help and hope that after this life was done, my daughter would be able to dance, just like the other little girls were learning at her age to do.

After I joined the church, I switched salons where I had been working. When I first started out, I was mostly cutting hair, but at this new salon, they did a lot of hair coloring and other services. I felt a little overwhelmed with it, so I prayed for God to give me wisdom, because I wasn't grasping all the new treatments. I turned it over to Him and let it go.

From that point, I went to all of the instructional classes that no one else would attend. I paid attention and read. It got to the point where I was so good at what I was doing that my boss and everyone at the salon came to learn from me and ask my opinion. That was the Lord's work in my life as He took me from not understanding to doing well and leading others. There is no doubt that the beauty industry is a bit on the rough side at times, but after I turned my life over to the Lord, it seemed that I always had other believers around to help guide me.

After I was attending the church for a while, I started going to their singles group. I met my second husband at the church through that group. We ran into one another regularly, and eventually I met his kids from his previous marriage. The group was called Celebrate Singles, but his kids would call our group "The Celibate Singles," and I would laugh and say that's what we were supposed to be. I went to all the events and met some really good friends there. I dove into all they had to offer.

The first or second year I was there, all the Pittsburgh Christian churches came together for a city-wide worship event at the Civic Arena. I felt good because I was hanging out with new people and not out in the world. I was slowly growing and understanding. At that city-wide event, two of our ACAC pastors were involved, along with different priests and pastors from various denominations in the community. They had the annual worship event for a few years after that, but eventually it lost momentum and I was sad when they stopped holding it.

At one meeting while were singing and worshipping, I said to my friend, "Oh my gosh, I'm so hot and woozy. What's wrong with me?" as I fell back into my chair. She told me it was the Holy Spirit working in my life. It gave me a picture of God cleaning and cleansing me for His purpose, and that made me want the Holy Spirit's presence even more. I was amazed by the overwhelming love and joy I felt.

We all went out to eat after one of those city-wide meetings, and Joe and I were at two different tables with Joe's back to me. He was trying to get my attention so he could talk to me, and that was the start of us getting to know each other. As I was finalizing my divorce, Joe would show up and try to help. As he was there to help support me, he got to know my daughter who would call him Uncle Joe—and still calls him that to this day. We didn't date as such, we just spent time at various events sponsored by the church. Eventually we married, and I fell madly in love with his children. We were married the day after Christmas in 2000.

Our first years together were okay, but I wouldn't say they were great. It was a big adjustment for Joe and me. I was thinking I could probably have children at that point, and Joe was 11 years my senior. I think he felt pressure to have more children, but I didn't know that at the time. Joe was still in a recovery process from leaving a church that he had attended with his first wife, and that church had a culture that tended to control people's lives.

I want to make this about what I went through in getting to know the Lord as I confronted my own weaknesses, and therefore I am hesitant to share much more about Joe. Many people at my church know and love him. He had his problems and, as you can read, I certainly had mine. Today, Joe is a good father to his children and is very involved in their lives. Maybe one day he will write a book and tell his story. I hope he will grant me grace if he does, and I want to give him grace as I tell mine.

We soon discovered that Lydia, my second daughter, had a lot of emotional problems as described in the previous chapter, and that she suffered from a recessive metabolic disorder. Her dad and I both carried the same recessive gene, a similar situation to my first marriage—although the effects were different. That was more difficult to deal with than anything I went through with Sam. I attended program after program and did a ton of research to learn about her condition and how to care for her.

When Joe and I first separated, he moved into my brother's house and paid a reasonable rent, for my brother knew we were going through a tough time and wanted to give us a break. My brother was in the Army and was serving in Kuwait and figured he had found someone who could watch over his house. Joe tried to do what he could while we were separated, but it got to the point that I needed to make our separation official. I couldn't live under the constant financial uncertainty.

The transition was difficult and challenging with many strange things happening. One time, the kids went to a low-end hotel near Pymatuning, a rural vacation spot north of Pittsburgh, and brought back bedbugs in their suitcases, which was a nightmare. On another occasion, we went through a time when the kids had scabies. I have no idea how all this stuff happened to us, but it was part of living life in the middle. Some of what we experienced was demonic with no natural explanation. At times, I barely slept due to worry and fear. I was constantly digging down into my faith, trying to seek God's help through all of it. I went through a lot of counseling at church.

On two occasions, I had to have a break from dealing with so many difficult situations and I ended up in the hospital suffering from depression, once while we were still married. I wasn't working any longer and was a stay-at-home mom. I eventually joined a divorce recovery group and it was a godsend for me, for I never felt judged there. The members understood what I was going through. They even helped me move when someone secured and drove my moving truck.

I sought pastoral counseling and was looking for guidance; I wasn't looking for direction on whether or not to get divorced. I just needed some support and help, which they, along with my mentor at the time, Angeles, gave me in abundance. Joe and I were finally divorced in or around 2010, and my church was supportive and non-judgmental.

Eventually, I moved into my brother's house with the kids, and it was a fight to get them into the new school district after we left the City school system. I had to argue with the school district to have the needs of my daughters met and it was tedious, but I did it. I had many therapists, specialists, and nurses coming in and out of the house to care for my kids. I still wasn't working; my job was all about caring for their needs.

My first husband remarried a couple of times after our relationship. When he lived in the city, he would come get Sam every other weekend or so, but I was still her main caregiver.

Then he got a job out of state as a truck driver. After going through his third divorce, he wanted to get back with me, but I said I couldn't do that. Joe is involved with the two younger kids a lot, which we will talk more about later.

I didn't know then that God was preparing me to help people as I am today. When I tell people that I know what they are going through, I really do. When I share my stories, it helps them have confidence that I can help. More importantly, it helps them know that God will help them, for He is the One who helped me.

I lived in our house for almost a year while Joe lived at my brother's house. When I said I couldn't pay the mortgage any longer on the house where I lived, I moved into my brother's house in 2009 and Joe moved back into the house. I'm still living at my brother's house today, but I am hoping to move in the near future.

I got my children established in the new school district, and I had all of the new therapeutic services coming there to that house. Samantha had a nurse who came to the house a few hours every day to work with her and tend to her medical needs. The wrap around services that included behavioral specialists and support people to teach us skills to cope had come and gone. In the afternoon, when my kids were in the school, my mother called me with news that would change my family's life forever, and put me in the middle of another almost unbelievable situation I never dreamed was possible.

Chapter 8

The Call That Changed My Life

The day was November 5, 2009. My mother called and had an urgent tone when she ordered me to turn to any national news channel. She told me there had been a shooting at Fort Hood in Killeen, Texas, where my older sister, Wandy, had just been sent before being redeployed to Iraq. I had learned only the day before that Wandy was there. Mother said the news was reporting there had been a shooting on the base, and that people had been killed.

Mother informed me that she had talked to Wandy's husband, who was in Baltimore, and he said that Wandy couldn't be near the place of the shootings because she had just arrived. He reasoned that Wandy was not due to be processed for another day or two according to the processing schedule for all the units that had been transferred to the base. In the meantime, my oldest niece, Wandy's daughter, called my mother and was of course quite upset as she was watching all of the reports.

Then my mother called back to tell me that my brother, who was also in the service and stationed in Illinois at the time recovering from shoulder surgery, explained to my mother how big Fort Hood is and said there was no way Wandy could be involved. My mother can be rather dramatic, but my brother advised her to calm down. Mom asked if she could come and spend the day with me, so I went and picked her up. She had the television on while I was fixing dinner and one of the children's therapists was present along with Sam's nurse. Mom brought a couple cans of beer with her that my brother left at her house. She sat watching television while she was drinking a can of beer. Her nerves were on edge, to say the least.

As the day went on, I told my mother to keep me informed. Of course, they weren't saying much about anything in the early hours after the shooting. It got to be around 9 PM and Ginger, Samantha's nurse who is still a good friend of mine, was finishing up with her and offered to take my mother home. The house had quieted down and the television was on, but I had the sound turned down.

My girlfriend, Lori, and I were catching up on the phone and talking about different things when I saw President Obama on the news. I asked my friend to pray for our family and told her that we hadn't heard anything. Two minutes later, I was about to go to bed when the phone rang. By then, it was a bit past 10 PM. It was my mother on the other end of the line, and she was screaming.

She lived in a high-rise building in which any visitor had to be buzzed in to come up to her place. She said there were two military officials downstairs in her lobby wanting to come upstairs to see her. She wouldn't let them in because she knew what they were coming to tell her. I screamed, took a deep breath, and told my mother she had to let them in. I told her that if she let them in, I would stay on the phone and talk her through whatever they were there to tell her. In the confusion, my mother hung up the phone.

I began trying to find someone to watch my children so I could go over to Mom's. Then she called back and kept screaming, "She's dead, he killed her!" The officers were still there and they wouldn't leave. I said I would be there as soon as I got the kids settled. I could not get hold of Joe, so I called his son, Brandon, who had just returned from active military duty in Iraq. He came right over to watch the children.

I rushed to my mother's and I saw the two officers standing there like statues, not moving. Mom was crying, bent over the table, and I went over and hugged her. We just held each other for a while. I had questions for the officers and they gave me as much information as they could. I told the officers it was okay for them to leave, since they weren't permitted to leave until they knew we were going to be able to move forward and handle the news. Then my sister Donna arrived right after they left. I think my sister brought a Bible I had given her. I sat on a Lazy Boy chair with my mother sitting on one of my legs and my sister on the other. My sister kept giving me the Bible and saying, "Read, Tammy. Read. I have to make sense of all of this. Read."

I read, prayed, and stayed till it was late. My sister spent the night after I went home. That night, I got in the shower and screamed out in prayer, asking God to reveal to me if my sister was with Him in heaven. I asked Him to please reveal to me what her eternal status was. Of course, I didn't sleep much and got the kids off to school but didn't mention anything to them. Then I went down to my mother's and Priscilla, my youngest sister, was there, so all three of mom's local surviving daughters were with her. Peggy, our other sister, lived out of town.

I called the church and left my pastor a message, telling him my sister was one of those killed at Fort Hood and to please have the church community pray for us. The next thing I knew, people from the church were arriving with food and calling, asking what they could do. I told them we would be at my mother's house and to bring any food there. My mother said she didn't want anything, but I said we would need something. People brought grocery bags full of food and also prepared meals.

Naturally, the Army kept calling and my mother finally asked me to handle the calls. When someone is killed in a situation like that, or even if they die overseas, the Army assigns the family a Casualty Assistance Officer (CAO) to walk with the family through the whole funeral process. This CAO must be the same rank as the soldier who was killed. Since my sister had the highest rank of anyone killed, Lieutenant Colonel, it took them days to find someone, for there aren't very many of them around. It seemed like we were dangling forever. The media were calling wanting interviews, our family was asking questions we could not answer, and we didn't know what the next steps were. As a family, we just needed to be and stay together.

The officer they eventually found was actually from the Seven Springs area of Western Pennsylvania. Meanwhile, I kept calling the social worker at the Army center to get information. The news channels kept calling, wanting to talk to us, but no one was ready for that. On the second day after Wandy's death, we had the news on to find out what was going on, because we didn't know what was being reported. We still didn't know what had happened, why it had happened, who survived, or who did the shooting.

The news was able to get hold of one of our family member who lived out of town, and she told them things about my sister that weren't quite accurate. We were watching the news and heard that erroneous information being reported, and it made everyone livid. I suppose that was the family member's way of dealing with the shock and grief, but it added to everyone else's pain.

The next morning, a lady from the Army called while I was still in bed. It was quite early and she told me they had located a CAO, Lieutenant Colonel Samuel Wagner. Finally, he called and we arranged a time for him to come meet at my mother's to start the process of handling all the arrangements. Lieutenant Colonel Wagner informed us that President Obama would be attending a memorial service in four or five days at Fort Hood. He inquired if we wanted to go, saying that the Army would pay for my mother, her spouse, and two of her daughters to go.

When I told Ginger, my nurse friend who had taken Mom home right before we heard the news, that I wasn't sure if I could go or if I even wanted to go, she said something I will never forget: "All I know is certain events in life, you don't ever want to look back and regret you didn't go or do." That was the confirmation I needed that the Lord wanted me to go. I told Joe and the rest of the family that I was going and they would have to make arrangements for the children, and I went.

Before I could go, I had one more difficult thing to do and that was to tell my children that their Aunt Wandy was gone. I consulted with the children's behavioral specialist working with us in our home, and we came up with a plan together. She was there when I told them. I sat the kids down on the floor in a circle and we all held hands, explaining to them what had happened. They were young, they were bewildered and sad, but understood that it was something difficult because of how I presented the news. Then we prayed.

It was a humbling experience to go through this whole ordeal. When trauma like my sister's death occurs, any and all family dysfunction is put on high alert. Tense relationships only get worse, and that was the case with my family. Things were said that should not have been said. Insults were common, and anger was unleashed on unsuspecting and innocent parties. At times, all I could do was pray, and pray I did.

Things were intense, and we almost missed our flight to Texas. Our CAO had to announce to everyone in the security line at the airport who we were, asking if we could go to the head of the line to make sure we didn't miss the flight. Everyone quietly and with reverence stepped to the side. It warmed my heart to see how much they cared about our family and honored our country and service people.

We flew into Killeen, and as soon as we arrived, we saw many others waiting for people who were coming to town for the memorial. We were informed by the Lt. Colonel that two gentlemen who shared some ending moments with my sister wanted to talk to us if we wanted to do that. Of course, we did. My niece Melissa and I eventually went to talk to them privately. They shared some of the things they remembered with us, and it was as if they needed to share with us as much as we needed to hear from them.

The people we talked to were a military ambulance crew who happened to be passing by the processing center when the shooting occurred, so they were the first ones on the scene. They told us a graphic story of how they held Wandy, actually dragging her out from where she was. As they did, they had a chance to speak with her.

Wandy directed them to tell us, her family, that she loved us. The crew told us how brave she was, telling them to go tend to other people. Wandy was a nurse practitioner in the psychiatric field and she wanted others to be cared for first. Wandy was at Fort Hood preparing for her second tour of duty overseas. During her first tour, she was on what's known as a triangle effect tour of duty.

Being a nurse practitioner in the psychiatric field, she prepared wounded patients mentally and physically after they were injured to come home from Iraq. She would help stabilize them in a medical unit in Germany. Then she would take the group who were well enough to come home to Walter Reed Hospital in Maryland. That's why they called it the triangle tour—from Iraq to Germany to the U.S. and then back to Iraq.

Between the first and second tour, she and her husband moved down to Havre de Grace, Maryland. Wandy got a position working at the Veterans Hospital near Baltimore. Since this was the first time women were on the ground in combat fighting, she prepared female soldiers to leave their families and children and then deal with what it took to come back home. Wandy had volunteered to go back to serve overseas, requesting this time that she stay on the ground in Iraq to better mentally prepare the patients to return home.

She had told me that she wanted to better prepare them for their homecoming and give them as much assistance as possible, whether they were injured or not. She had been training in Washington State for this latest assignment, and had been at Fort Hood for only 24 hours. She wasn't even scheduled to go through the processing center, but she went early because as a commander, she knew she wanted as much time as possible to mentally prepare the soldiers going out for the first time.

I had talked to her on the phone at times, but had not seen her for about a year and a half prior to her death. She had been stationed in so many places, including Hawaii, that it was hard to keep up with where she was. Therefore, we would just talk on the phone whenever our schedules permitted. Wandy was 54 years old when she died. Since she was 11 years older than I, she was my second mother, as I explained earlier. She took me everywhere with her.

We met with those military paramedics who were with her in her last moments in one of the conference rooms at a local hotel. That was a tough meeting. We were also assigned a military chaplain and met him at that hotel as well. First, the chaplain talked with us, and then the paramedics came in. I can't remember a lot of what they said, but I do remember it being really sad and comforting at the same time. I was there more to be a moral support for my two nieces and great nephew who were also present.

That night I held my niece, who was in her 30s, like a baby all night long as we sat and cried. The next day, when they had the memorial service, we were overwhelmed. It was right there on site at the base. They had big office spaces where the families could meet with all of the dignitaries before they proceeded with the memorial service. That was rather awkward for me, but people felt the need to greet and express their condolences to all of us.

Our chaplain was there, one of my sister's Army and war buddies was present, the Lt. Colonel, and our assigned driver. Every family had a van and driver to take us wherever we needed to go. Many people were excited that President Obama was coming, but it didn't do much for me. It was nice that my sister and these people were being honored, but I don't know how to explain how I felt. I could tell that the military personnel and the chaplains were excited about the President's visit. I was sitting on the chair and before the President came in, I whispered to the chaplain, "You think this is something? Just wait until our Lord Jesus comes back. This is nothing." He looked at me and said I was absolutely right.

The First Lady and the President passed by, and everyone was excited. They wanted pictures but it did not serve as a source of comfort to me. I just went with the flow. Don't get me wrong. I was grateful the President had made the trip, but at that point in time, I was pretty numb. We went down on the field, and they seated everyone, with the highest ranking officers on the front rows, then the dignitaries, and the rest of us. There were thousands of people there. I've never seen anything like it, and the media were everywhere.

The ceremony was quite well done. We were in south Texas so even though it was November, it was very hot and sunny. Before we had gone out, however, we were standing around making small talk, waiting and waiting. An older looking soldier with grey hair came up and talked with the Lt. Colonel, asking if we were the Warman family and requesting to have a word with us. The Lt. Colonel brought him to us, and he introduced himself as a Catholic chaplain, informing us that he had held my sister in his arms the last few moments of her life. She passed away in his arms.

The chaplain was certain that Wandy wanted us to know that she loved her whole family. Then he explained that the chaplain anointed Wandy with oil. Wandy knew she was dying because of her severe internal injuries. Then I asked him to repeat that for Wandy's daughters who were close by. My niece looked a little shocked and stunned, but I knew it was an answer to my prayer. God was telling me that Wandy was with Him.

I later found out that Joe had the children watch the entire memorial service, which was broadcast nationally. I was delighted that Wandy's nieces and nephew could view this service for someone who had been so special in my life. I wish they had had the opportunity to get to know her as I did, but that will have to wait for another time in another age, when not only Samantha is dancing, but we are all joyfully reunited in the presence of the Lord.

The bodies of the soldiers killed were taken to Dover for autopsies. As we pieced together what happened when Wandy was killed, we discovered that she was sitting next to one of the younger victims. Wandy realized what was coming and threw a young lady down and stayed on top of her. That was the story then, but we have heard different versions since. It is clear, however, that by whatever she did, Wandy saved some girl's life.

That night after the memorial service, we went to the hospital where the thirty people who were injured were being treated. We met with the young woman who was next to Wandy at the hospital, and she told us what happened. The following day we went home, and ironically, it was Veteran's Day. I wrote this tribute to those who serve on the plane coming home:

> *Leaving Fort Hood, I felt a sense of irony or even an unsettling turmoil within me, while checking into the Killeen-Fort Hood Airport on November 11th, which is Veteran's Day. Part of me didn't want to leave not knowing this country truly understood the depravity that occurred the day when my sister was violently gunned down along with twelve other of her colleagues.*
>
> *Attending the memorial ceremony were many*

soldiers who were injured who came to pay their respects to those who had given their lives just by doing their job, which was preparing for war. Only then did they realize that this war has no boundaries. They also wanted to pay tribute to the family members left behind. I was one of them and it was an indescribable surreal experience. My heart goes out to each and every family member as well. I can only hope and pray that this malicious act of cowardice by a man completely misinformed of who God really is will be turned into something positive. Perhaps families growing closer together, as mine has done that. A nation rising up above what is "the norm" to stand firm with absolute strength and fortitude to rid the uncertainty of terrorism or terrorist-like actions once and for all.

After the memorial service in the evening, my family was escorted by our CAO Lt. Col. Wagner, Lt. Col. Breedlove, my sister's army buddy, and Captain Palmer our chaplain. These fine representatives from our armed forces showed us much humility and respect, and I am extremely grateful for their kindness. We were taken to a hospital about 30 minutes away from the post and were told a story of a soldier who was seriously injured during the rampage. This story was significant and involved what happened to my sister.

The soldier's name was Staff Sgt. Joy Clark. She began her story by telling us in her own words exactly what happened. Lt. Col. Juanita Warman, my sister, saved her life. The details overwhelmed us. The comfort it brought to us seemed to help us start the healing process. Joy along with her family offered us their deepest sympathies and gratitude for my sister. My niece, Melissa, and my great nephew, Corie, and I were honored to be there with this brave soldier and her family grieving for the loss of Juanita.

We had a few somber moments only to realize a new bond of friendship and connectedness were sparked. We now had a common bridge bringing two families together. A testimony of one who is living with a new purpose in life. It was with much appreciation and humility that I said I was the one who was honored and felt the highest respect not only for Joy but for all the injured and whoever was involved in any way.

For them, the healing process will be slow and long with much suffering. I for one have a deeper admiration, love, and respect for them all. The bravery and selfless acts of heroism will probably never be expressed or told in a way that will be full understood unless one was there. I pray that no other soldier will ever have to find this out for themselves.

NEVER FORGET.

NEVER TAKE OUR FREEDOM FOR GRANTED.

NEVER, NEVER, NEVER GO WITHOUT SAYING TO THOSE WHO SERVE

OR WHO HAVE SERVED, "THANK YOU."

Mom had followed everything on television, and when

we got back, she was sad, depressed, and generally a wreck. Of course, we were all concerned about her. My sister was to be buried at Arlington Cemetery in Virginia, and it was a difficult time as we waited to find out when the funeral would be. We ended up having to wait a couple of weeks until the autopsy was completed. In military cemeteries, it's not like you can come and go as you please. There are time slots for they only permit so many funerals on any given day.

Wandy's funeral was actually expedited, but it was still a two-week time frame before we could hold it. Those two weeks were some of the toughest days of my life. There was such a sense of loneliness and a feeling like the bottom had fallen out of my world. I kept tabs on my mother, knowing she had to be going through trauma, too. After I got the kids in bed or off to school, I would scream out to the Lord in despair. I would be in prayer on the floor, in the middle of the afternoon, and those prayer times stand out in my mind.

Once I was lying on the floor in prayer and opened my Bible. Those were the darkest days I had ever known. In the midst of that darkness, the verse that jumped out at me was, "Your word is a lamp for my feet, a light on my path" (Psalm 119:105). I knew He was speaking to me. I then looked up and saw a lamp on in the room that I *know* was not on before I started praying. I jumped up and immediately started praising Him. I ran around the house singing His praises and thanking Him for His light and goodness. I was so touched and comforted that I got up and went about my normal routine since the kids were off to school.

I opened the blinds right after that, looked out the window, and noticed a coin between the screen and the window. I had never noticed it before, even though we had lived there for months. It was some sort of a coin with the image of an angel on it. I thought, "Oh my gosh, Lord, this is getting freaky." I don't know what happened to that coin, but I kept it for a while.

Two weeks later, the CAO rented a van and we all drove down to view the body at a funeral home in the Washington D.C. area, and then the burial took place at Arlington National Cemetery. This time, the entire family was there, including my mother. Our CAO assisted us with our special request to have the chaplain who helped us at the Texas memorial be present at the funeral. The Army wasn't going to pay for him to come since he was stationed in the Midwest, but we pushed and pushed for it, and didn't really want anyone else. That's how important it was to our family. There were a lot of people at the funeral, which was right before Thanksgiving.

A year later, there was another one-year memorial service. There was also a 5K race at Fort Hood to raise money for the Wounded Warrior Project, and I trained and ran in that. Eventually and only after some controversy, Wandy was awarded the Purple Heart medal. I have had the privilege of honoring my sister at many other events and parades. I had to step back from it all, however, because of family dynamics and that was fine with me.

A year or two later we went down to Arlington, where my sister is buried next to a major who was killed the same day. Quite a few of us were there, and by chance my brother-in-law, Wandy's husband, was also present. The major's family was also there next to us as well. Afterwards, we all went out to dinner together. That was uncanny and really quite special. Wandy's chaplain was in town and he was able to join us.

Before we move on, let me say again that this was what happened to the best of my recollection. Times were so chaotic and we were seeking so much information that it all started to jumble together. I would not be surprised if one of my family members remembers something being said that I do not, or remembers the order of things happening differently than I do. Unless you have been through that kind of shock, you may not understand how deeply it can affect your ability to think and retain information. Some of it is fuzzy and some of it is stamped indelibly on my mind. My main point I want to leave as we finish this chapter is that we all loved my sister, mourn her loss in our own way, and still process the pain according to how it works best for each of us.

Chapter 9

Still Living in the Middle

Now that I look back on my life, I can see that the Lord has been with me from a very young age, even though I didn't understand that or grasp the implications. As I have written this book, I have remembered a lot of things I had forgotten or come to realize I now see them in a whole new light. When I was quite young, we lived in a large house and I remember my mother sitting in the room with my siblings and me, reading us a children's Bible that was a picture storybook. For the first time in my young life, I wondered who this God was that she was talking about. That wonder returned every holiday or once in a while when I was watching TV.

I had a cousin and some friends in the neighborhood who went to Catholic school and we would have conversations. I would ask what it meant to go to their school and why they went. They were trying to teach me about God and I would ask questions. I always knew there was something for which I was searching. Years later, I would go into the closet in my room to pray. I don't remember anyone teaching me to do that.

When I did it, I sensed that He was always with me. When we were kids, my sister, who is two years older than I, was quite mean to me and I thought it just had to be evil, otherwise it didn't make any sense. I look back now and know that He was with me the whole time, and that gave me peace, even when I was a child. Over the years, my relationship with the Lord has grown to the point where He is my Lord, but we are also friends.

All this didn't come together until I gave my life to the Lord and became part of my church that I have mentioned throughout the book, Allegheny Center Alliance Church. That's been my home and my family. I have not simply attended services there, I have built relationships there, first with the Lord, and then with His people. I didn't simply attend, I got involved in many of the ministry outreaches the church had. It's happened to me more than once that someone has come up to me, and told me that something I said or did a while back was special to them when it happened. I didn't even know their name or remember the occasion but they did. That speaks to the kind of relationships I have had with people at my church.

It was often difficult to get my children ready to attend the church because of the special care they required before and after we left the house, not to mention their often unpredictable transitional behaviors. It was a priority for me because coming to church was my only sanity and chance to step away from my circumstances to be fed spiritually and connect with other people. I needed people with whom I could share and speak—people who were grounded and mature in the faith. I had to get close to that because I was hungry for it. It's all I wanted and still want.

My oldest daughter, Sam, will be 23 by the time this book is published. When she was younger, I would bring her to the prayer room where people would pray over her. Leaders would approach me to say that she was ministering to them, encouraging them through her gentle way. That inspired me, and taught me that I had something to give others that could help them, no matter how difficult or challenging my situation was. The same was true for Sam.

Sam was brave and enjoyed church. Once when she was eight years old at a summer camp, the counselors helped her climb up a zip line and she did it, even though she could barely walk. Then the leaders said, "If Sam can do it, I can do it. Who am I to be afraid?" I looked at them as they told me that and thought, "Wow, thank You, Lord!" As she got older, to be honest with you, our church didn't have a lot of programs for special-needs children. I don't fault them, for I searched around the city and found that not many churches had anything special for children like my Sam. There was a lot of heartache over that lack, and I tried to advocate and even volunteer to help make some things happen. Unfortunately, there were times when I wanted to get away from my situation so I could receive some help that was just for me.

Sam didn't really fit in with the students in high school, so she stayed with the middle schoolers a lot. Many people had a good heart and wanted to include her in various activities, but I would have liked to have seen more things specifically geared toward her. Having said all that, Sam comes every week to church. Now she lives in a group home and they faithfully bring her.

It's so special that Sam lives in a group home now. One of the reasons she doesn't want to live at home is so she can make her own choices. It's difficult sometimes for me to allow her to do that because I had to do it for her for so many years. We made the choice together for her to be on her own, and it felt right. The home offers job coaching and Sam has a job. They care for her and look after her medical needs, taking her to all her appointments, because I couldn't do all of that with my current job and ongoing family responsibilities with my other children.

Also, I have to work and I couldn't leave her at home alone for hours at a time. I am grateful she is in a safe environment, and her home is nicer than my home. She has a roommate and there's a full staff. They take her to community events and anywhere she wants to go. She has a boyfriend, which is another story.

My Lydia and Westin live in two different homes. Lydia's a daddy's girl and daddy treats her quite special, so of course she wants to be with her father. I have grown to accept that. Westin enjoys being with dad and craves his attention. Lydia is doing much better these days, and I believe it's the best she can do. Lydia also loves to come to church and enjoys the interaction. In spite of her autism, she likes to come to social events and be invited to participate in other things. She loves singing in the Urban Impact Choir, and enjoys being a part of that. I was praying a few years ago and felt the Lord tell me she would be known for her praise of God, and that's what has happened. She goes with her dad to Catholic church and enjoys doing that because she likes doing whatever her dad does.

Lydia has less services and therapy than a few years ago, but she's doing well. There's never going to be perfection in her situation, unless she's cured completely with a miracle, but she's come a long way. She has her seizure disorder, so we still have to go to the professionals for all the tests, medications, and all that comes with that. People who see her say that she is a happy and fun girl. Again, mental challenges are so different for the people who raise those who are afflicted with them.

Westin prefers not to come to ACAC. He attends a Catholic school and goes to church with his dad. I am glad he goes to church somewhere. When the girls were growing up, I would often say I didn't know what it was like to be a soccer mom, for that wasn't part of our lifestyle. Now I am proud to say that I know what it's like, for Westin loves soccer and is a very good player. I go to all his games and I am his biggest cheerleader. Only time will tell how growing up around so many challenges will affect him and his life choices. I pray for him, and know that God will guide him in the path that has been chosen for him to walk.

As I begin to bring this book to a close, I have my Bible open, searching my notes and notebooks for special verses or events that helped me get through and build my faith. I mentioned earlier that my family wanted a boy, and then I was born with my twin brother. I always carried a sense that I was less important and that caused me to seek attention. Then I read Jeremiah 1:5, which states, "Before I formed you in the womb I knew you, before you were born I set you apart." I understood when I read it that God saw me in my mother's womb and had a plan and purpose for me.

Of course, through all my trials and mistakes, I have clung to two other verses: "For I know the plans I have for you," declares the Lord, "plans to prosper you and not to harm you, plans to give you hope and a future" (Jeremiah 29:11), and "We know that in all things God works for the good of those who love him, who have been called according to his purpose" (Romans 8:28). Those verses are basic, but they have meant a great deal to me.

When I was single, when the children were more than I thought I could handle, those verses kept me going. Now, God is my friend, and I talk to Him constantly, to the point that if anyone looked in my car while I am driving and sees only me, they think I'm either crazy or on the phone.

I have been asked to speak at a few gatherings for ladies, especially after my sister's death. It was special to see how God was with me in the middle of that ordeal and how He revealed Himself to me as evidenced by the peace I had. The Bible says that kind of peace is unexplainable and it is. My church was praying for me during the ordeal with my sister's death, and many people sent cards and other expressions of support. When I was at Fort Hood, I talked to our church secretary, Sheran White, who has also experienced much personal loss. She helped me tremendously. There were low points for me in the weeks following my sister's death and people ask me about my attitude toward her shooter. I have no unforgiveness, and have actually wanted to write and tell him I forgive him.

In some ways, my family's experience and reaction were more difficult for me than the actual event. It was easier to forgive the shooter than it has been to forgive family members. Some people can relate to that I hope. I will be honest and say that I have dealt with self-pity for the longest time. I would console myself by telling myself there was a reason for it all. I am not sure if that's a coping mechanism or a faith practice.

I have read through books about people who experienced tragedy and I would think, "Do I need to be angry at God like this person was? Do I need to get it out?" I tried that, and it may be where some people are at, but it wasn't an issue for me. I just accepted it, and was all about trying to move forward. I continue to make mistakes. I don't want to dwell on it, for I'm afraid I will never recover from the downward spiral.

I know Sam wants to get married. Part of me is excited about that, but the other part of me is fearful and concerned. I recently had to turn that over to the Lord because her boyfriend has special needs, too. He suffers from Prader-Willi Syndrome, and a person with that Syndrome tends to make it all about him or her. I am delighted to report that he is improving and his relationship with Sam has been a very positive thing for him. Obviously, I want Sam's happiness.

When Sam was young and I received her diagnosis, I had to research it and we didn't have the Internet. I went to the library and the doctor gave me medical stuff to read. I reread her diagnosis countless times, looking up the technical words, because it was written in medical jargon. I learned that her disorder was comprised of three components: cerebral palsy with its intellectual challenges, cognitive delays challenges, along with her skin disorder. It comes with a lot of other traits, but those are the three main ones. When I read that, I thought, "It's not going to be easy, but we will work on the physical."

My main concern was the intellectual. I remember lying face down on the floor and praying, "Lord, if You say this is what it is, I pray for grace and mercy when it comes to that." Considering her disability and what the challenges could be, her problems are mild when compared to others. I hope and pray that she can think through things and make the right decisions.

For my Lydia, the miracle will be that she can get through life without being victimized. My prayer is that her anger and aggression will subside when it comes to family and loved ones, especially towards me. I pray that she grows up to a level of maturity and won't remain in an adolescent state of mind. I hope she can go to college. It's been difficult when family members talk about all the wonderful things their kids are doing, things like cheerleading, softball, college, or modeling. I'm just happy when my kids get through the school year.

Westin is my unexpected blessing. I love the fact that he tells me all the time he wants to be an aeronautical engineer. He is smart enough to do that, and I get compliments all the time about his manners with adults. He loves the attention and really wants to be a gentleman. He has been through a lot already in his young life, and my prayer is that he learns to put God first in every aspect of his future.

As I have mentioned earlier in this book, I relate everything to what I now do for a living, which is family support. When I meet with families through my job, I tell them I will stand with them through it all because I understand where they are and much of what they are experiencing. I share my story and allow them to relate it to theirs, which helps them accept me for who I am and what I am trying to do with them.

I am someone who has been through it and they're not alone. I encourage everyone I work with to find a support group. My support network came through my faith and church. If they say there isn't a group for them, then I encourage them to start one. I constantly had to try to help people understand what I was going through and what my children were experiencing. It wasn't easy, and still isn't for me or for the families with whom I work.

I can say, without a doubt, that today I have more love and grace for circumstances not understood by most. There were times when I felt judged by an attitude that said, "Why doesn't that woman do something with or for her children?" or from Christians, I have heard, "There must be sin or not enough faith in that woman's life for that to be happening." I tell families

72

today that I know what it's like to have very few people understand what they are going through. It was not only with my
children, but in light of my marriages.

At times, I have written poetry to try and stay sane. I have
some ideas for children's books, which is where this book project got started. Obviously, it moved beyond a kids' book to this.
One of my poems goes like this:

> *Wearing the sandals or shoes of Jesus.*
>
> *Walk a mile in someone's shoes with Jesus.*
>
> *The situation many times would mean no condem-
> nation but mere compassion through felt empathy.*
>
> *How can we be Christians called to help people
> in any situation if we only judge and not wear the
> shoes of those hurting and struggling, without walk-
> ing the footsteps of the afflicted?*

As Christians, we are called to help and support those
who are at a low point. Sometimes, from my low point, I feel
people are looking down on me. I remember going through a
difficult period once, and I kept hearing the same message: God
wasn't going to give me what I couldn't handle. There was one
day when I felt like smacking the next person who said that to
me. I struggled with that and finally took it to the Lord in prayer.
The Lord showed me that everyone was telling me half the truth,
for He would not send what I could not handle, but to handle it
I had to give it to Jesus to carry on my behalf.

It has taken me years to accept who I am, regardless of
what everyone else thinks. Even now, I have a lot of help and
support, and I am in a good place. I am still in the middle of
things, but I am seeing a Christian counselor, and learning how
to do my job more effectively. There are moments I still feel I

have to work through my shame, but she helps me work with that. I just pray that the Holy Spirit in me would rise above that and remind me of who I am in Christ, that I am just like anyone else.

In 2000, when I was new in the faith and struggling with my life situation, Angeles, who I mentioned earlier as my mentor and friend, came to me after a church service. She told me she had been in prayer and thinking of me, when the Lord impressed her with a passage from Acts 9:15-16:

> "But the Lord said to Ananias, 'Go! This man is my chosen instrument to proclaim my name to the Gentiles and their kings and to the people of Israel. I will show him how much he must suffer for my name.'"

I knew the Lord was telling me something through Angeles, and it was that I was going to suffer but also be used for him. I believe that is happening now with and through my job, and through this book. My suffering has helped others, so His promise was true, but it took a while for it to happen.

If you are reading this and you are going through the unspeakable, through something you did not think would ever happen to you, then be encouraged today. If no one understands what you are going through, God does. I urge you to have a talk with Him, and unload your burdens on Him. Take these words of Jesus to heart as you seek Him:

> "Come to me, all you who are weary and burdened, and I will give you rest. Take my yoke upon you and learn from me, for I am gentle and humble in heart, and you will find rest for your souls" (Matthew 11:28-29).

Find a local church and get involved. If you don't know

where to go, then get in your car like I did and trust that God will lead you. As difficult as these days may be for you, they will pass and will ultimately make more sense than they do now.

If you are reading this and you don't feel like you are going through anything close to what I have been through, if you don't know what it's like to live in the middle, I encourage you to find someone close to you who is! You probably won't have to look very long or hard, and when you find that person, creatively devise a way to support and help them. In John 9, the disciples came upon a blind man who had been blind from birth. The disciples asked Jesus: "Rabbi, who sinned, this man or his parents, that he was born blind?" (John 9:2). The disciples wanted to engage Jesus in a theological discussion, but Jesus would have none of it. He responded with these words:

> "Neither this man nor his parents sinned," said Jesus, "but this happened so that the works of God might be displayed in him. As long as it is day, we must do the works of him who sent me. Night is coming, when no one can work. While I am in the world, I am the light of the world" (John 9:3-5).

Jesus was telling them, "Don't try to figure this situation out. See it as an opportunity to serve God by serving the needs of others while the light is on that situation and you see it clearly." This may require you to get your hands dirty, to lose some sleep, or to be around a situation that makes you feel helpless or awkward. If that's the case, don't run away. Embrace the opportunity and do what you can with what you have.

I still feel like I am living life in the middle—in the middle of my children's situation, in the middle of my own failures and brokenness, in the middle of many cases at work that don't seem to be close to resolution. I am in the middle of family, of life, of work, and of my walk with the Lord. I am learning that the middle is a good place to be in, for it gives the Lord a chance to carry me when I don't have the strength to do it.

As we close, I thought I would look up the word middle in the gospels and look at what I found:

> "Later that night, the boat was in the **middle** of the lake, and he was alone on land. He saw the disciples straining at the oars, because the wind was against them. Shortly before dawn he went out to them, walking on the lake" (Mark 6:47-48, emphasis added).

> "When they could not find a way to do this because of the crowd, they went up on the roof and lowered him on his mat through the tiles into the **middle** of the crowd, right in front of Jesus" (Luke 5:19, emphasis added).

> "There they crucified him, and with him two others—one on each side and Jesus in the **middle**" (John 19:18, emphasis added).

From those three passages, I see that living in the middle is not such a bad place, and it was where the Lord seemed to be on more than one occasion. If that's where Jesus is, then that's where I want to be. I accept the middle position (in fact, I am the middle child!), and will continue to make the most of every opportunity as I live life in the middle! Thank you for reading, and may God bless you where you are today!

Postscript

As this book was going to press, I got a promotion at work! I am now a supervisor in the family-run organization I work for. I see this as God's promotion because someplace along the way, I did indeed learn some lessons and now I have a heart to share them. This is new territory for me, so I am learning to rely on the Lord and draw on His grace even more than in the past. God is faithful, and He will be faithful to you as well.